BOOK SOLD
NO LONGER R H.P.L.
PROPERTY

RICHMOND HILL
PUBLIC LIBRARY

SEP 15 2006

OAK RIDGES MORAINE
905-773-5533

CATHEDRALS
AND THE CHURCH

PATRICIA LEVY

A⁺
Smart Apple Media

First published in the UK by Franklin Watts
96 Leonard Street, London EC2A 4XD

Produced by Arcturus Publishing Ltd.
26/27 Bickels Yard, 151-153 Bermondsey Street, London SE1 3HA
Copyright © 2004 Arcturus Publishing Ltd.

Series concept: Alex Woolf
Editor: Clare Weaver
Designer: Chris Halls, Mind's Eye Design Ltd., Lewes
Illustrator: Adam Hook
Picture researcher: Glass Onion Pictures

Published in the United States by Smart Apple Media
2140 Howard Drive West, North Mankato, MN 56003

U.S. publication copyright © 2005 Smart Apple Media
International copyright reserved. No part of this book may be reproduced in any form
without written permission from the publisher.
Printed and bound in Italy

Library of Congress Control Number: 2004104272

ISBN 1-58340-572-0

9 8 7 6 5 4 3 2 1

RICHMOND HILL
PUBLIC LIBRARY

SEP 15 2006

OAK RIDGES MORAINE
905-773-5533

Picture Acknowledgements: Akg-images/Schutze/Rodemann 21; The Art
Archive/Bibliotheque Municipale Reims/Dagli Orti 5/Musee des Arts Decoratifs
Paris/Dagli Orti (A) 7/University Library Prague/Dagli Orti 9/Dagli Orti 10,
19/Canterbury Cathedral/Dagli Orti (A) *cover*, 14/Bodleian Library, Oxford
20/Bodleian Library Oxford, Canon Class lat 81 folio 137r 17/British Library
22/Canterbury Cathedral/Jarrold Publishing 27/The Art Archive 28/Galleria deli
Uffizi Florence/Dagli Orti (A) 29; Bibliotheque Nationale, Paris 12; Bodleian Library,
Oxford MS.Bodl.264, pt.1 24; The British Library/HIP 13; Topham Picturepoint 23.

CONTENTS

THE CHURCH AND THE MEDIEVAL AGE

Pope Adrian IV

Adrian IV was the only Englishman who became a pope. Here, a friend recalls how difficult it was for him to do the job:

"He used to say that no one is more wretched than the Roman pontiff [the pope]. . . . Even if he had no other problems, the weight of his duties alone would overwhelm him. He confided to me that he had found so many cares in the cathedral of Peter [in Rome] that by comparison all his earlier troubles seemed like joyful moments and happy times. He added that were it not for fear of opposing the decision of God he would have preferred never to have left his native England. . . ."
(From Medieval Worlds: A Sourcebook, *edited by Roberta Anderson and Dominic Bellenger)*

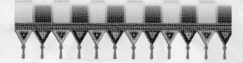

The extent of Christianity by the 12th century A.D.

Christianity is a religion that follows the teachings of Jesus Christ, a man who lived in Palestine 2,000 years ago. At that time, Palestine was a part of the Roman empire. Today, there are many different branches of Christianity, but in the medieval age most of these branches had not developed. Christianity in the medieval age meant the Church, and it was an essential part of life for people throughout Europe.

Across the Roman empire, in the centuries after the death of Christ, usually given as A.D. 30 or 33, the numbers of his followers had grown slowly. At that time, the Roman empire extended from England in the north to parts of northern Africa in the south, and from Spain in the west to what is now Iraq in the east. At first, though there were groups of Christians in the major cities of the Roman empire, there was no central organization to the Church. However, the religion gradually developed its influence until, by the 10th century, the Church had become a wealthy and powerful institution, ruled by men called bishops.

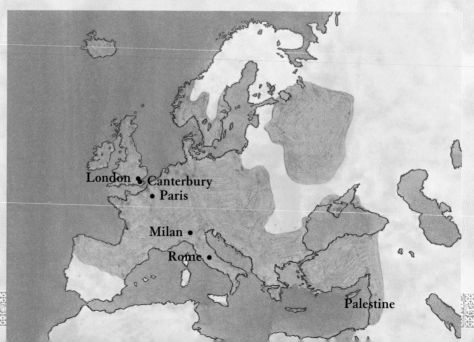

London • • Canterbury
• Paris

Milan •

Rome •

Palestine

The Church was involved in all aspects of the lives of the people of the Middle Ages, from regulating the daily conduct of the people to investing a king. Here, bishops crown the king of France.

The central organization of the Church was in Rome. The bishop of Rome was, and still is, called the Pope, and he became the leader of the other bishops. The Pope made all the final decisions about matters to do with the Church. He also had a special power to release people from the consequences of committing sins (breaking the laws of the Church). Sins could include general crimes, such as murder, as well as special Church crimes such as heresy, the refusal to accept the teachings of the Church.

Each of the old regions of the Roman empire, which had begun to break up in Europe in the fifth century, had its own bishop. The center of power for these bishops was based in the largest town of the region. Each bishop ruled over a diocese, an area of land that made up a collection of smaller churches called parishes. The more powerful bishops, based in the larger and more important towns, became known as archbishops. Some bishops also held the higher rank title of cardinal, which meant that they helped to decide who was to be pope.

Ecclesiastical Courts

The Church in Rome operated its own courts, known as ecclesiastical courts. Church laws governed most people's lives just as much as the general laws of their country did. Church law covered marriage, the care of children, usury (the lending of money for a fixed charge), legal contracts that involved the taking of an oath, and the payment of special taxes to the Church, called tithes. The Church could punish people with fines or physical punishment; at worst it could expel wrongdoers from the Church, a very serious punishment called excommunication.

CHANGES IN THE CHURCH

Church Building

For about 300 years, from the beginning of the 11th century, a wave of church building took place throughout Europe. Cathedrals—special churches where a bishop was in charge—became bigger, and new parish churches were built. Many of these buildings no longer exist, but it is known that from 1050 to 1350, several million tons of stone were quarried in France to build 80 cathedrals, 500 large churches, and tens of thousands of parish churches. In England and France there was one church for every 200 people. More stone was quarried in France alone than the amount ancient Egyptians had used throughout the centuries of pyramid building.

Because the Church was so influential, powerful people fought for control of it. Until the 11th century, bishops, and even popes, were often chosen by kings. This meant that the king could appoint a bishop who would do what he was told, and the king could control what happened to church incomes. Another problem that many Church leaders faced was corruption within the Church. As the Church became richer, popes failed to establish firm rules for the behavior of Church leaders. Bishops became very wealthy and powerful men who enjoyed privileged lives. In 1073, the new pope, Gregory VII, had very strong views about the way in which the clergy should conduct their lives, and about who should appoint the bishops and other clergymen. From the time of Gregory's rule, Church leaders were usually appointed by the pope or by a group of cardinals. The bishops in their turn appointed the parish priests and other clergymen who worked for them. This meant that the Church had better control of its

A bird's-eye view of the large, self-contained Benedictine monastery at Cluny, France.

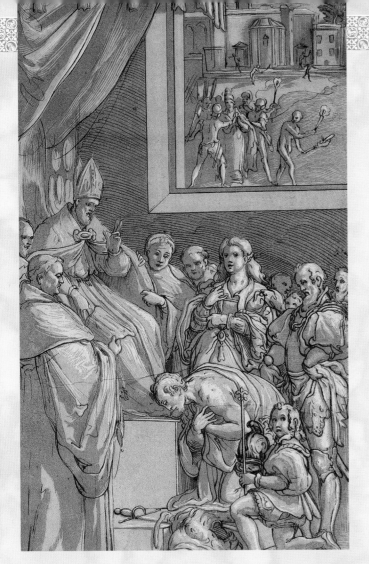

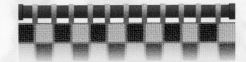

An influential man with sincerely held views about the role of the Church, Gregory VII had an enormous influence on the Church for generations. Here he is shown blessing King Henry IV of Germany.

own money, and this gave it more independence. Gregory also laid down strict rules of behavior for clergymen, including the rule that they should not marry.

Gregory's reforms led to other important developments within the Church. From the early years following the death of Christ, people who had felt very close to their religion had joined monasteries, places where they could dedicate themselves to prayer. Monasteries first became a part of Christianity in western Europe in the sixth century when groups of monks, called Benedictines after their founder St. Benedict, settled in Italy. After the changes made by Pope Gregory in the 11th century, many more monasteries were built. The reforms not only gave monasteries greater freedom from the interference of kings but also encouraged ordinary people to join them.

A Lordly Bishop
A contemporary clergyman disapproves of a corrupt bishop:
"This Anthony Bek [1283–1311] was second to none in the realm, save the king only, in pomp and bearing and might of war, busy rather about the affairs of kingdom than of his diocese, a powerful ally to the king. . . . To him it was a small thing that the greatest earls and barons . . . should kneel before him, or that, while he remained seated, knights should stand long and tediously before him like servants. Nothing was too dear for him if only it should magnify his glory. He bought cloth of the rarest and costliest and made it into horse cloths. . . . He was never in want and abounded in all things unto the day of his death."
(*From* Life in the Middle Ages, *G. C. Coulton)*

THE CHURCH AND SOCIETY

Pope Urban's Speech to the Knights of Europe:
"If you wish to be mindful of your souls, advance boldly, as knights of Christ, and rush as quickly as you can to the defense of the Eastern Church. . . . Under Jesus Christ, our Leader, may you struggle for your Jerusalem, in Christian battle line . . . that you may assail and drive out the Turks . . . and may you deem it a beautiful thing to die for Christ in that city in which He died for us. But if it befall you to die this side of it, be sure that to have died on the way is of equal value, if Christ shall find you in His army. God pays with the same shilling, whether at the first or eleventh hour."
(From The First Crusade: The Accounts of Eyewitnesses and Participants, *August C. Krey)*

A crusader sets off for the Holy Land, ready to give up his life for the Church.

It is difficult for people today to understand just how important the Church was to ordinary people in the medieval age. From birth onwards, people's lives were governed by the Church. The Church controlled special events for young people, called confirmation, as well as people's marriages. Death was another matter for the Church, with special prayers and burial practices.

People generally believed that their behavior while they were alive would determine their destination after death. They thought that those people who died without committing any

The leader of the Hussites, Jean Huss (1373–1415), a peasant from Bohemia, became very influential and was burned at the stake as a heretic. His death caused war in Bohemia.

Heresy

Besides Muslims (also called the Saracens), there were other people, called heretics, who were seen as a threat to medieval Christianity. Heretics were Christians who questioned whether Church beliefs and teachings were true. This challenge to the Church was called heresy. One such group were the Cathars, who believed that everything material—wealth, property, even everyday necessities—was evil. The Hussites were another group who refused to recognize that the Pope was the head of the Church, or that only priests could carry out the important religious services. Early on in the medieval period these groups were tolerated, but later they were persecuted by special courts, called the Inquisition, and hundreds of people were burned to death for heresy.

sins would go to heaven, while those who died without seeking forgiveness would go to hell. They also believed that confessing their sins and asking for forgiveness would grant them a shorter stay in purgatory, a special place where those who died went in order to pay for sins that they had confessed to while they were alive.

One way in which people thought that they could reduce their time in purgatory was to contribute money to the Church. Rich men, from kings to noblemen, as well as rich town merchants, provided the money to build magnificent cathedrals. In this way, they thought, they could pay for their sins and also gain power and influence while they were alive.

An example of the enormous power that the Church had over ordinary people can be seen in the Crusades. These were a series of invasions of Islamic lands that Christians regarded as sacred to their religion. In 1095, Pope Urban II made a speech urging Christian knights to wear the sign of the cross and take back what Christians called the Holy Land. Thousands of men of all classes set off to fight, many of them never to return. They believed that what they were doing was the will of God and that taking part would guarantee their place in heaven.

CHURCH BUSINESS

The Importance of Holy Relics

Holy relics were highly prized items in medieval times. A very wealthy man, a king or baron, might have his own personal collection, and churches kept their collections securely locked up. The relic might be the entire remains of a saint or just a fragment of his finger bone, the water a saint's corpse might have been washed in, or a fragment of what was claimed to be the cross on which Christ was crucified. One medieval source tells the story of St. Hugh of Lincoln who attempted to steal part of a relic from a monastery in France by biting off a piece of a female saint's finger.

Churches before the medieval age were places where ordinary people tended to go only at Easter, when they were expected to confess their sins and take part in a ritual called communion. The growth of religious belief in the medieval age changed all that. Churches became the heart of the community.

The medieval Church was very much involved in the daily lives of its parishioners. The parish priest was expected to supervise a number of rituals—listening to confession, baptizing babies, blessing marriages, confirming the faith of young people, providing spiritual aid to the dying, and overseeing the burial of the dead. Everyone was expected to attend the ceremony called mass, which took place on Sundays. The Church was also the main source of education for ordinary people. People learned Bible stories from stone carvings and the paintings that decorated church walls. People were taught the penalties of sin and told they would be judged by God after they died.

In the San Guiliano Convent in Italy are the relics (cloak and purse) of St. John of Capistrano (1386–1456).

These pilgrims are visiting the shrine of a saint, perhaps to ask for a cure for an illness. Pilgrims collected badges at each shrine they visited in order to display their piety.

The Church year began with the 12 days of Christmas, celebrating the birth of Christ. This festival was later followed by Shrovetide, and then Holy Week, which commemorated the death and resurrection of Christ and was the most important religious event of the year. Church processions took place and everyone was expected to take part in the ritual called Holy Communion. Summer was marked in the Christian calendar by Corpus Christi, a celebration of the Church belief that Christ was bodily present in the bread taken at mass. This was also accompanied by religious processions. Finally, the year ended with All Souls and All Hallows, when the Church held prayers for the souls of the dead.

Another big business for the Church, especially in the cathedrals and grand town churches, was pilgrimages. In medieval times, people believed they could be cured of illness if they touched a holy relic. Pilgrims to a shrine that contained the relic of a saint would donate money to the church in exchange for a cure. On a particular saint's day, the church holding a relic of the saint would be crowded with pilgrims.

The Value of a Relic
This passage describes the efforts of people trying to get a piece of clothing from a dead saint as her body is carried to the church for burial:
"The whole people flocked together and rushed upon the sacred body with incredible ardor so that the guards could by no means keep them at arm's length. Before the procession had reached the church three tunics had been cast upon her for each in turn was cut into piece. . . . The soldiers, who did all they might to defend her with swords and maces, could scarce hinder the people from cutting her body itself into pieces in their excess of devotion."
(From Life in the Middle Ages, *C. G. Coulton)*

A PEOPLE'S CHURCH

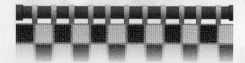

Marriage

In early medieval times, the Church was not involved in the marriage contract, but people usually exchanged their promises of loyalty at the front door of their local church. After these exchanges, they attended a mass inside the church. In 1200, the Church in England ordered that in the future the priest should be present at the exchange of vows: "And let not any marriage be contracted unless there is a threefold proclamation in the church, nor if the persons are not known. And let persons not be joined in matrimony unless publicly in the face of the church with a priest present. If it is done otherwise, let them not be admitted anywhere in church without special permission of the bishop."
(*From* Medieval Worlds: A Sourcebook, *edited by Roberta Anderson and Dominic Bellenger*)

Here, sometime around 1400, the Bishop of Paris blesses the fair at Lendit, near the city.

Besides the official role of the Church in the lives of ordinary people, there were other, more practical matters expected of the priest. The priest was often the only person in the parish who could read and write, so he would assist in any legal problems of the parishioners. He would be called on to settle disputes, bless the crops, and administer the business of collecting tithes. Many pagan rituals, from the time before Christianity, had become part of Christian festivals, and priests accepted these as a way of keeping control over people's lives.

In many areas, the parish church may well have been the only building of any substance, and probably the only one built of stone. The cathedral was as much a meeting place as it was a place of worship. The main body, or nave, of the church (where today there are rows of benches for the congregation) was unfurnished in medieval times. This provided a big, multipurpose, open space. Guilds—associations of craftsmen or

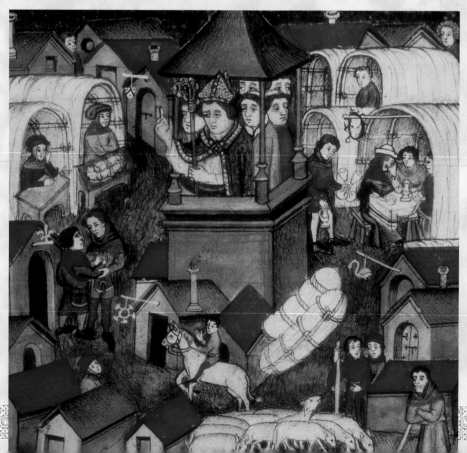

An important part of the job of a Church leader in the Middle Ages was to bring converts into the Church. Here, an adult is baptized. Among those already converted to Christianity, baptism took place at birth, so this man is probably a heathen.

tradesmen—held their meetings in their local church. Records show that banquets were held in cathedrals, because in 1358, they were banned in an English cathedral after complaints about excessive overeating. In the summer, mystery plays (stories about the life of Christ) were performed in many cathedrals.

Some cathedrals were even used for fairs or markets. At Troyes, France, month-long champagne markets were held around the city's churches, and goods were put into the church storerooms for safekeeping. Salisbury Cathedral, in England, hosted a horse fair for a time, both in the churchyard and in the building itself. Even St. Paul's Cathedral in London was, in the 14th century, used as a marketplace and as a place for drawing up legal contracts. It was common all over Europe to use the parish church at harvest times for threshing the corn, and later for storing it.

King John and the Church
It seems likely that the majority of the people of medieval Europe were members of the Church and looked to it for guidance in their daily lives. It is interesting, however, that between 1208 and 1214, following a dispute between the Pope and King John of England, the Pope banned all religious services in England. Although there are many records that survive from this period, very few of them suggest that the absence of church services had any effect on ordinary people.

CATHEDRALS

Some Cathedral Terms
The *nave* is the central area of the church where the congregations stood in medieval times.

The *chancel* is the eastern end of the church where the priests and the choir stand. It is divided off from the nave.

An *apse* is a circular extension on the main body of the church. It often holds a private chapel. In early churches, the chancel was a simple apse.

The *clerestory* is a series of ornate windows on the first floor of the nave, above the roof of the aisle. It allows light into the body of the church and meant that there could be many stained-glass windows.

The *transept* is an aisle that crosses the church at the east end in front of the chancel. In Gothic churches, it extends into two extra rooms at the north and south of the church, making the building cross-shaped.

A 13th-century stained-glass window from Canterbury Cathedral.

The Church in medieval Europe was divided into administrative areas called dioceses. At the head of each diocese was a bishop, and his administrative center was the cathedral. It was usually the largest and most magnificent church in the diocese. Cathedrals all over Europe were built in cities because only the cities were wealthy enough to build on such a large scale. But in England, there were other cathedrals, such as Canterbury, Winchester, and Worcester, which were staffed by members of a religious order, such as monks, and these were often built within a monastic site rather than in a town.

Early medieval cathedrals were simple stone structures, built in a style called Romanesque, because they had architectural features that were learned from the Romans. They have rounded arches on doorways and windows, and a rounded

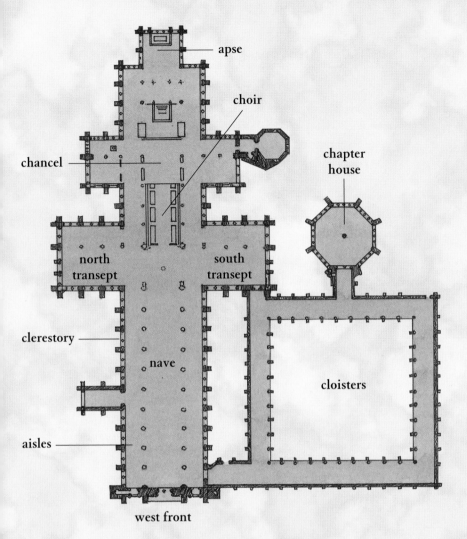

apse

choir

chancel

chapter house

north transept

south transept

clerestory

nave

cloisters

aisles

west front

This diagram shows the layout of Salisbury Cathedral, begun in 1220. At the south of the building are the cloisters, a covered walkway where monks could walk and meditate, and the chapter house, where business was conducted.

A Description of Lincoln Cathedral
"With proud boldness the wall soars up towards the clouds and the roof towards the stars. The vault seems to converse with the winged birds; it spreads broad wings of its own and like a flying creature jostles the clouds. . . . Handsome jointing arranges there in seemly rank a thousand shafts which strong, precious, and gleaming render the whole structure of the cathedral durable with their strength while enriching it with their costliness . . . for the shafts stand soaring and lofty, their finish is clear and resplendent, their order graceful and geometrical, their beauty fit and serviceable."
(*From* The Cathedral Builders of the Middle Ages, *Alain Erland-Brandenburg*)

chancel. These were the first cathedrals with large, high naves, whose purpose was to hold a large congregation of ordinary people. They were basically square buildings with a chancel at the east end where the mass was said. Later in the medieval period, aisles were built along the sides of the nave for people to walk up to the altar, and a third aisle was added to cross the nave in front of the altar. Later still, side rooms called apses held smaller chapels, each with its own altar holding the sacred remains of a saint. As architects grew bolder, they built high towers for the church bell and complicated arched pillars, called clerestories, in the side walls of the nave. This style is known today as Gothic. It is characterized by a cross-shaped building, rather than a simple rectangle, and it has much more elaborate archways and pillars, with a lot of open spaces to let in light.

BUILDING A CATHEDRAL

An Inspector's Report on the Structure of Chartres Cathedral

Chartres Cathedral in France was begun during the 12th century. Almost 200 years later, the church officials worried that it was in danger of collapse and commissioned some famous architects to report on its safety:

"First: we have seen the vault of the crossing; repairs are necessary there; and if they are not undertaken . . . there could be great danger.

Item: we have seen the flying buttresses; they need pointing up, and if this is not done at once, damage may ensue.

Item: there are two piers which support the towers which need repairs."

The list continues. The repairs must have been good ones, since in modern times Chartres is considered Europe's best preserved Gothic cathedral.

(*From* Cathedral Builders of the Middle Ages)

When a cathedral was built, the most important person was the patron. This was the person who commissioned the cathedral and found the money to pay for it. Kings, bishops, abbots, lords, and even whole city councils took on the role. Sometimes, it took hundreds of years to build a cathedral because the patron died or the cash ran out. The building of Milan Cathedral in the late 14th century was administered by a committee of as many as 300 people.

After the patron, the next person of importance was the architect. He drew up the plans for the cathedral and oversaw its building. Architects were often master masons, men who had learned stone masonry and sculpture as an apprentice. They traveled around Europe, learning new techniques and taking new designs with them. Later, medieval architects

A great cathedral often took many years to build. The workers on the site had the use of quite complex machinery, as shown in this artist's impression of a building site.

16

This 15th-century illustration shows a cathedral being built in Italy. Stonemasons can be seen at work, cutting up large pieces of stone.

Flying Buttresses

Architects began to discover ways of making their buildings taller and more elaborate, building wide naves with vaulted stone roofs. These buildings quickly grew beyond the point where the outer walls could support the weight of the masonry, and other ways had to be found to keep the building upright. One option was the flying buttress. This was an arch-shaped support, which stood against the outer walls of the building. By the end of the medieval age, these buttresses often had three or more tiers, taking the support higher and allowing for even taller, wider buildings. Occasionally, there were accidents with ceilings collapsing, such as the ceiling vault of the church of Cluny Monastery, in France, which collapsed in 1120 during the building process.

specialized in just one aspect of building (for example, staircases or towers), and several architects worked on each project.

Alongside the architect was a team of stonemasons. The masons sourced the stone, cut it themselves, made their own tools, carved the stone into the desired shapes, and set it in place. To do this they had simple winches and cranes for lifting. Scaffolding was built into the walls as the building rose, and walkways along the scaffolding were made of woven basketwork. To accurately create the fine detail in carved pillars, patterns were drawn out on a stone or plaster floor, and the stone to be carved was set on it.

Working alongside these master craftsmen were other skilled workers: carpenters, mortar mixers, blacksmiths, and plasterers. Records show that skilled masons often earned twice as much as the plasterers, who in turn earned more than the unskilled manual workers, the water carriers, hod carriers, carters, and general laborers.

CATHEDRAL DECORATIONS

Medieval Clocks
Mechanical clocks are a medieval invention, and early ones were the most complex pieces of machinery yet known. They were also extremely expensive to make, and only very wealthy places, such as monasteries or cathedrals, could afford to have them made. A metal face showed the time, and mechanical figures might move to strike the hours. Clocks were at first kept inside the cathedral, where only the clergy could see them, and their only function was to make sure that services were held at the right time.

The medieval cathedral had no seating, heating, or light beyond candles, but it was a riot of color, from the brightly painted walls, statues, and ceilings to the huge stained-glass windows.

To the east of the nave was the chancel, separated from it by an ornately carved wooden or stone screen. In the chancel was the altar. Inside this were the remains of a saint whose presence made the altar holy. The remains would have been held in a specially made container, called a reliquary, which was covered in precious stones. Many rich men gave the church gifts in the hope of forgiveness for their sins, and so

Even the simplest of churches in the Middle Ages contained silver or even gold objects, such as this chalice for holding the altar wine.

the medieval chancel became filled with silver and gold chalices and other instruments used for the mass. Also inside the chancel were the carved and decorated bishop's throne and the stalls for the choir.

At the west end of the cathedral was the font, a carved stone basin that held holy water. Over the years, a collection of monuments and tombs accumulated around the walls of the nave. They were dedicated to the wealthy men who supported the church. They were often carved from alabaster or marble.

Unlike today, the inside walls of medieval cathedrals were plastered and brightly painted. The paintings might illustrate stories from the Bible, saints' lives, or stories that warned what would happen to sinners. The most interesting aspects of the thousands of surviving wood and stone carvings are the variety of stories to be found carved upon them. They include scenes from rural life, strange animals, human faces, and even figures of the men who built the cathedral, from mortar mixers to hod carriers to the architect himself.

The outside of the cathedral was even more imaginatively carved. Every opportunity was taken to decorate the exterior, from rooftop gargoyles spouting rainwater to figures of the saints over the door. The west entrance of the cathedral was always the most highly decorated. In time, even architectural features such as the flying buttresses became elaborately carved, looking more like delicate wings than supports for the walls.

A Disapproving Voice

Not everyone in the Church approved of the increasingly ornate and gorgeous objects which began to decorate cathedrals. Here is the opinion of one senior Church leader: "I put on one side the vast height of the churches, the excessive length, the empty spaces, the rich finish, the curious paintings. We will look rather at the sumptuous ornaments encrusted with gems and gold, put there that money may breed money and pilgrims may give to monks the alms that should be bestowed upon the true poor."
(From Medieval Worlds: A Sourcebook, edited by Roberta Anderson and Dominic Bellenger)

Mechanical clocks, such as this one at Wells Cathedral, England, were first constructed in Europe toward the end of the 13th century. Few individuals could afford one, and they became part of the display of wealth in churches.

CHURCH MUSIC

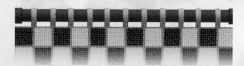

Christmas Celebrations at Cluny Monastery

A quote from Peter the Venerable, 12th-century abbot of Cluny Monastery: "It is the custom of Cluny to celebrate the savior's nativity with singular affection, and with more devotion than any other solemn feast; not only with melody of song, with longer lessons in church, with the light of multitudinous tapers, but far beyond all this with special devotion and copious shedding of tears, in joyful unison with the angelic Host."
(*From* Life in the Middle Ages, *G. C. Coulton*)

The earliest church music was a simple chant, known as the Gregorian chant, that accompanied religious services. Monks sang the words of the service without any other musical accompaniment. In the early part of the medieval age, the choir consisted entirely of clergymen—monks or priests employed in the cathedral. Later, this caused problems as the Gregorian chant grew more complicated. Monks weren't always the best singers and, besides, they could not always be available for the service. By the middle of the period, the Church had begun to employ ordinary people to sing in the choirs. Only men and boys were allowed to join the choirs. Some cathedrals and monasteries such as Rome; Metz, in Germany; and St. Gall, in Switzerland, had choir schools where boys learned the profession. And at Wells Cathedral, an entire village street, which in medieval times was the home of the choir of the cathedral, still survives. Sometimes, rivalry broke out between cathedrals over a particularly good chorister, and occasionally choirmasters resorted to kidnapping.

This 15th-century illustration shows a group of monks singing together. At the borders of the picture are laymen, studying texts, illustrating the idea that ordinary laymen could read the scriptures.

The bells of the village church in Saintes-Maries-de-la-Mer, in southern France. The simple 12th-century church not only has this complex set of bells, but it contains holy relics said to have belonged to the Virgin Mary's sister and the mother of Saints James and John, who, legend says, fled to this place in the year A.D. 40.

The first organs were placed in cathedrals in the 10th century. They were very simple machines with levers rather than a keyboard, and they were intended for use during processions to add to the grandeur of the event rather than to accompany singing. By the 11th century, organs had keyboards and were small so that they could be carried to where they were needed.

It is unlikely that other musical instruments were used in the medieval church service, although cathedral decorations often include pictures of angels playing instruments. Even more curiously, there are many carvings of animals playing instruments, such as the bagpipes or the organ. This may be because the Church believed that secular music was sinful.

Another form of music was church bells. In their simplest form they were a single note, intended to tell the congregation that it was time to come to church. Early medieval bells were simple metal tubes, which were struck rather than swung. By the 13th century, the shape of the modern bell had been invented, and people had discovered that the size and proportions of the bell determined the sound it made. This meant that several bells could be hung together to make a tune when they were rung in a certain pattern. Bell manufacture became an important trade, and bell foundries flourished.

The Bells of Ely Cathedral
In the 1340s, the bells of Ely Cathedral in England were replaced, and the account sent by the manufacturer to the bishop has survived. Besides the cost of the charcoal, the molds, the labor, and the rope, the account records the names and weights of the bells. Bells were given religious names and their weight recorded. A hundredweight (cwt) is equal to 113 pounds (51 kg) and a pound (lb) is equal to 0.45 kg.
Christ - 37 cwt 92 lbs
John - 27 cwt 4 lbs
Mary - 21 cwt 41 lbs
Walsyngham – 18 cwt 4 lbs

CATHEDRAL ADMINISTRATION

Cathedrals and Funerals
The funerals of powerful men, such as bishops, were conducted in the cathedrals. The coffin was covered in velvet cloth often embroidered in gold and was frequently topped by a wax effigy of the deceased. It was placed in the center of the nave and surrounded by mourners dressed in black cloaks. A wooden frame was built above the coffin to hold candles. Beside the coffin lay the bishop's vestments, or official clothes. The body would finally be laid to rest in the cathedral grounds or in the crypt. In medieval times, people believed in the Day of Judgment, when bodies would be resurrected, so the body was prepared for that day.

The coronation of Richard I in 1189. This picture shows the procession on the way to the cathedral.

Medieval cathedrals were almost certainly the biggest employer of people in their regions. The city cathedral employed members of religious orders to assist the bishop in the administration of the diocese, run the cathedral school, and to take part in the religious service each evening. Besides the clergy, the cathedral employed many more people to maintain the church building, carry out the daily running of the church, and look after the cathedral grounds.

The monastic cathedrals were part of a very complex community. Some were more like small towns. Besides the monks who spent their daily lives in prayer or study, the monastery would have had its own land and its own serfs to farm it.

se les ordoinance du sa   et autres en chappes de draps

Some tithe barns, such as this one in Widdington, Essex, still survive into modern times.

The Coronation of Richard I
The medieval historian Roger of Hovedon describes King Richard I's coronation: "When the duke (Richard) had come to the altar, in presence of the archbishops, bishops, clergy, and people, kneeling before the altar, with the holy Evangelists placed before him, and many relics of the saints . . . he swore that he would all the days of his life observe peace, honor, and reverence towards God, the Holy Church, and its ordinances. . . .
Then Baldwin, archbishop of Canterbury, pouring holy oil upon his head, anointed him king in three places, on his head, breast, and arms, which signifies glory, valor, and knowledge, with suitable prayers for the occasion. . . . They then clothed him in the royal robes . . . after which the archbishop delivered to him the sword of rule, with which to crush evildoers against the Church. . . ."
(*From* Roger of Hoveden: The Annals)

Within each diocese were many smaller churches. Each of these churches paid tithes, special Church taxes, to the cathedral to contribute to its upkeep. These churches, in their turn, collected tithes from its congregation. A small village church would have its own living, a farm which provided the parish priest's income. In addition, the priest could expect to receive payments for each baptism or marriage. Many villagers paid their tithes in kind rather than cash, and there are several tithe barns still in existence which were built to hold the grain paid to the church as tithes. The parish priest was aided by one or more curates, young priests who were learning their trade and waiting to be given a parish of their own.

MONASTERIES AND ABBEYS

The Monastic Life

"When you wish to sleep, they wake you, when you wish to eat, they make you fast. The night is passed praying in the church, the day in working, and there is no repose but in the refectory; and what is found there? Rotten eggs, beans with their pods on, and liquor fit for oxen."
(*From* Medieval Britain, *Lloyd and Jennifer Laing*)

Small numbers of monasteries existed in Europe long before the medieval age. After the reforms of Pope Gregory in the 11th century, a new sense of devotion began to emerge in Europe, and many people began seeking such monasteries. The biggest monasteries were called abbeys, while their smaller branches were called priories.

Every monastery had a cloister, a covered passageway where inmates could study and work. There would also have been a refectory where the monks ate, a hospital, a grain store, a bakehouse, a pottery workshop, offices for tanners, weavers, brewers, guest accommodation, a home for old people, gardens, water mills, and beyond these a farm run by the monastery and worked on by monks and peasant workers. The farm would include water mills, a blacksmith, storage barns, stables, and animal housing.

In the early days of the monasteries, life was harsh. The monks or nuns lived lives of fasting and poverty and enjoyed few comforts. They took vows of celibacy, were strictly vegetarian, and spent their days and nights in strict rituals of prayer and work. Some orders even took vows of silence.

This illustration shows medieval nuns and monks playing with a bat and ball, and not engaged in their religious duties.

Their work might include toiling in the fields, creating illuminated manuscripts, teaching, or bookbinding. Monasteries were, for hundreds of years, centers of art, literature, and science.

Later, however, the monasteries became very wealthy as people donated land and money, and the regulations became less harsh. Meat was allowed in the diet, and monks were able to employ more peasants to work the land. Both the monasteries and the communities of nuns kept horses, and pleasures such as hunting with hawks and, in the case of nuns, buying fashionable clothes became common. However, one order of monks, the Franciscans, took their vows of poverty very seriously and owned no land, going about their countries begging for alms.

One of the reasons why the monasteries became less dedicated to religion is because for centuries it was the custom to recruit new members as children. These children were called oblates and were given to the monastery by their parents along with a donation of money or land to cover their upkeep. It was an honor for a family to have a child become an oblate, and families saved up money for that purpose. It meant though that many of the inmates of the monasteries had no real calling or inclination to be a monk or a nun. By the end of the 12th century, this practice was banned, and only genuinely committed adults were admitted.

Most monasteries had their own fields, tended to by the monks.

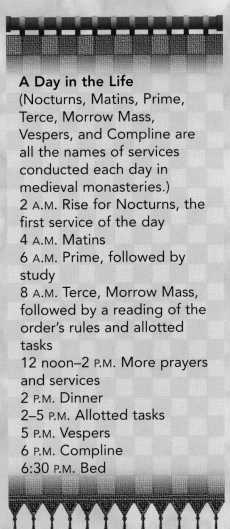

A Day in the Life
(Nocturns, Matins, Prime, Terce, Morrow Mass, Vespers, and Compline are all the names of services conducted each day in medieval monasteries.)
2 A.M. Rise for Nocturns, the first service of the day
4 A.M. Matins
6 A.M. Prime, followed by study
8 A.M. Terce, Morrow Mass, followed by a reading of the order's rules and allotted tasks
12 noon–2 P.M. More prayers and services
2 P.M. Dinner
2–5 P.M. Allotted tasks
5 P.M. Vespers
6 P.M. Compline
6:30 P.M. Bed

HOLY GROUND

Memorials

Few medieval tombs remain in medieval churchyards, but those inside the churches have survived. Most of these belong to distinguished members of the church or important members of society. Their memorials focus on what they had done during their life to justify being remembered. Hughes Libergies, the architect of Rheims Cathedral, in France, is shown on his tombstone holding a model of the cathedral. Some are more creative. The tomb of John Stanley in Elford, England, shows him holding the tennis ball that killed him. Toward the end of the medieval age, when a terrible plague had killed hundreds of thousands of people across Europe, tombstones began to reflect an obsession with death. Tombstone carvings showed the rotting corpse that lay beneath, and inscriptions warned the living to be aware of their own impending death.

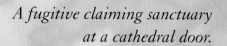

A fugitive claiming sanctuary at a cathedral door.

The grounds of the cathedral formed a special area around the church where much of the social activity of medieval life took place. In English cathedrals, the area around the church was called the close. It was a piece of open land around which the various other buildings associated with the church (such as the bishop's palace, houses for other clergymen, and the churchyard itself) were grouped. The immediate area around the church building formed the churchyard and was the burial place for ordinary citizens. In the period between 1208 and 1214, when church services were banned in England, churchmen were forbidden to conduct burials. There are stories of coffins being hung from trees in the churchyard until they could be buried later.

The churchyard had other functions, too, besides the burial of the dead. In the great cathedrals, which were important to pilgrims, stalls were a permanent part of the churchyard. The stalls sold badges, flasks of holy water, and oil so that the pilgrims could carry them home from their trip to show that

The tomb of Edward, the Black Prince, at Canterbury Cathedral. He was legendary for his chivalry, and replicas of his armor hang over his tomb.

The Black Prince
"Such as thou art, sometimes was I,
Such as I am, such shalt thou be.
I little thought on th'oure of death,
So long as I enjoyed breath.

But now a caitiffe poore am I,
Deepe in the ground, lo here I lie,
My beautie great is all quite gone,
My flesh is wasted to the bone."

Written on the tomb of Edward, the Black Prince (1359–76), son of Edward III and heir to the English throne, at Canterbury Cathedral, in England.

they had made the journey. Some churchyards contained high crosses on which Bible stories were carved, a way of communicating with people who could not read. The church door, or sometimes the churchyard gate, was the site for medieval weddings.

The churchyard was also used for many less-sacred activities. Although trading on Sundays was banned by the Pope in 906, fairs were often held in churchyards on Sundays. During All Hallows, pagan practices such as putting out food for the dead were still carried out in graveyards. May Day and Midsummer's Day in England were often celebrated by building tents of green leaves against the walls of the church and performing plays beneath them. It was 1240 before dancing at cemeteries was forbidden at Worcester Cathedral, England.

For criminals, another useful part of the cathedral grounds was the sanctuary knocker on the door of the cathedral. Once a person who was being hunted by the authorities reached this door and took hold of the knocker, he could not be arrested.

THE END OF AN ERA

For centuries, the Church led the way in the arts, philosophy, architecture, science, and technology. But as the medieval period drew to a close, new ideas began to challenge the views of the Church.

Throughout the Middle Ages, the Church had controlled learning and writing. But in the middle of the 15th century, the printing press was invented. By 1500, about six million books had been printed in Europe, more books than had been made in the whole of the rest of the medieval period put together. Books now included alternative ideas about medicine and science. People were able to rediscover and reassess classical works of Greek and Roman philosophy, unfiltered by the doctrine of the Church.

For many years there had been criticism of the Church, especially its wealth. People became dissatisfied with the Church because it seemed to be more concerned with collecting tithes and selling indulgences (forgiveness for past sins in exchange for money) than looking after the souls of its people.

The Black Death

In the 14th century, a terrible plague spread across Europe. In some areas it killed as many as two-thirds of the population. Some historians have seen the plague as part of the movement from medievalism to the humanism of the 16th century and later. With smaller populations, people were forced to develop new technologies to survive, they began to question the teachings of the Church that could offer no help against the disease, and they turned to other sources for help and education.

The figure of Death stands triumphantly, watching over victims of the Black Death.

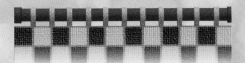

In 1517, Martin Luther published his criticisms of the sale of indulgences. Luther believed that forgiveness could not be bought. He thought that people could be forgiven for their sins only if they really felt repentance. His criticisms were published and spread quickly across Europe. Luther had intended only to reform the Church from within, but the resulting controversy led eventually to the Reformation and the creation of two branches of the Church—Roman Catholicism and Protestantism.

Other events also began to influence people's lives. In 1488, Bartholomew Diaz, a Portuguese explorer, sailed around the Cape of Good Hope, discovering the extent of Africa for the first time. In 1492, Christopher Columbus reached the New World (the Americas). This, along with the rediscovery of classical ideas about politics, ethics, the arts, and much more, began the process by which ordinary people turned away from the Church for their solutions and began to look at the world around them in a new way, uncluttered by the demands of the Church.

Some of Luther's Criticisms
In 1517, Luther published 95 statements concerning the sale of indulgences, which he pinned on the church door at Wittenberg, Germany. Here are some of them:
"21: Those preachers of indulgences are in error, who say that by the Pope's indulgences a man is freed from every penalty, and saved.
24: The greater part of the people are deceived by that indiscriminate and high sounding promise of release from penalty.
32: They will be condemned eternally, together with their teachers, who believe themselves sure of their salvation because they have letters of pardon.
43: Christians are to be taught that he who gives to the poor or lends to the needy does a better work than buying pardons.
52: The assurance of salvation by letters of pardon is vain."

Martin Luther (1483–1546), painted around 1529 by Lucas Crunch. Luther was a simple Augustinian monk, but his ideas led eventually to the beginnings of Protestantism.

29

TIMELINE

1020	Building work on Chartres Cathedral, France, begins.
1072	Lincoln Cathedral begun.
1073	Pope Gregory VI's reforms to the Church.
1079	Winchester Cathedral begun.
1083–89	Building of Ely Cathedral.
1087	St. Paul's Cathedral in London burns down and rebuilding begins.
1093	Building of Durham Cathedral begins.
1095	Pope Urban II encourages men to begin the Crusades.
1095–99	The First Crusade.
1096	Norwich Cathedral begun.
1098	The monastic order called the Cistercians is founded.
1110	The earliest record of the miracle plays in England.
1120	Part of Cluny Cathedral, France, collapses.
1147–49	The Second Crusade.
1174	Canterbury Cathedral burns down and is largely rebuilt.
1187	Muslim armies capture Jerusalem.
1189	Richard I is crowned King of England.
1189–92	The Third Crusade.
1192–1235	Wells Cathedral is built.
1202–04	The Fourth Crusade
1208–14	All religious services in England are banned by the Pope.
1210	The Franciscan order is founded.
1220	Salisbury Cathedral is begun.
1240	Dancing is banned in the cemetery of Worcester Cathedral.
1264	The festival of Corpus Christi is celebrated for the first time.
1340	Ely Cathedral commissions a new set of bells.
1347–50	The first outbreaks of the Black Death.
1358	Banquets are banned in Exeter Cathedral.
1361	The second outbreak of the Black Death.
1376	Death of Edward, the Black Prince.
1414	The leader of the Hussites is burned at the stake.
1453	Constantinople falls to the Turks.
1478	The Spanish Inquisition begins.
1487–98	Portuguese voyages of discovery begin.
1492	Christopher Columbus discovers America.
1517	Luther publishes his criticisms of the Church.

GLOSSARY AND FURTHER INFORMATION

All Souls, All Hallows Christian festivals celebrated in autumn.

baptism A religious service where someone, usually a baby, is officially brought into the Christian Church.

Byzantium The eastern section of the Roman empire consisting of areas of southeast Europe and Asia Minor, with the city of Constantinople as its capital.

cardinal An important figure in the Church hierarchy, who helped to choose the new pope.

celibacy Not marrying or engaging in sex.

clergyman Someone who has taken vows to be a member of the Church.

Confession A ceremony in which a parishioner tells his priest all the sins he has committed in recent days.

confirmation A special ceremony conducted when Christians are teenagers. They confirm their belief in Christianity.

Corpus Christi A summer Christian festival that celebrates the belief that the body and blood of Christ are present in the mass.

corruption When someone in a position of power, such as a bishop or a king, uses his power for an immoral purpose.

Crusades A series of military expeditions with the aim of breaking Muslim control over what was seen as Christian Holy Land in the Middle East.

diocese An area of a country ruled over by a bishop.

divine right The belief that kings or emperors ruled with authority granted to them by God.

excommunication The decision by the Pope to refuse someone the right to take part in church services or have any dealings with the Church.

gargoyles Stone carvings of imaginary creatures placed over a rainwater spout on the roof of a cathedral.

heresy Religious beliefs which do not agree with those of the Church hierarchy.

hierarchy A system of grades in authority.

Holy Communion A name for the moment when a Christian eats the bread and drinks the wine that represent the body and blood of Christ.

holy water Water that has been blessed by a priest.

Holy Week The week surrounding Easter Day that recognizes the death of Christ by crucifixion.

humanism The name given to a way of thinking that followed after medieval philosophy. It focused on the human, secular things in life, rather than on the ideas of the Church.

indulgences Letters from the Pope forgiving someone for his sins.

Inquisition A special court made up of priests who investigated heresy and put on trial anyone suspected of witchcraft.

Last Judgment The ancient Christian belief that on the last day of the world everyone will rise from the grave and be judged by God.

mason A person who builds using stone.

mass A religious service in the Catholic Church. Bread and wine represent the body and blood of Christ, and each member of the congregation eats a piece of the bread and drinks some wine.

medieval age The period of European history between the fall of the Roman empire and the fall of Constantinople in 1453.

Middle East The area covered by the land between Egypt and Iran.

monasticism The culture of monasteries where people live a life of prayer and withdrawal from society.

mortar A mixture of lime and sand that is used to cement stone blocks together.

mystery plays A series of plays telling the story of the life of Christ.

reliquary A container made of precious metal in which a relic or some remains of a saint or Christ are kept.

Roman empire The control of Europe and part of the Middle East under the authority of Rome between 31 B.C. and A.D. 476.

sacraments Religious rituals that had to be conducted by a priest.

secular To do with the everyday life of people rather than their religious beliefs.

tithes One-tenth of a person's produce that had to be given to the church each year.

winch A machine that helps to lift heavy things.

RECOMMENDED READING

Caselli, Giovanni. *The Middle Ages*. New York: McGraw-Hill Children's Publishing, 1993.

Hart, Avery, and Paul Mantell. *Knights and Castles*. Charlotte, Vt.: Williamson Publishing, 1998.

Langley, Andrew. *Medieval Life*. New York: DK Publishing, 2000.

McAleavy, Tony. *Life in a Medieval Abbey*. New York: Enchanted Lion Books, 2003.

RECOMMENDED WEB SITES

http://www.btinternet.com/~timeref
http://www.learnhistory.org.uk/medieval
http://www.learner.org/exhibits/middleages/morelign.html

INDEX